W9-AJQ-319

THE TALE
OF SUNLIGHT

GARY SOTO

UNIVERSITY OF PITTSBURGH PRESS

THE TALE OF
SUNLIGHT

MIDDLEBURY COLLEGE LIBRARY

ABW 5502

1/1989
Am Lit

Published by the University of Pittsburgh Press, Pittsburgh, Pa. 15260
Copyright © 1978, Gary Soto
All rights reserved
Feffer and Simons, Inc., London
Manufactured in the United States of America

Library of Congress Cataloging in Publication Data

Soto, Gary.
   The tale of sunlight.

   (Pitt poetry series)
   I. Title
PS3569.072T3   811'.5'4   77-18743
ISBN 0-8229-3375-6
ISBN 0-8229-5293-9 pbk.

PS
3569
072
T3
1978

Acknowledgment is made to the following periodicals for permission to reprint poems that appear in this book: *The Nation, Paris Review, Poetry Northwest, Revista Chicano-Riqueña, The Seneca Review,* and *The Slow Loris Reader.*

"The Point" appeared in *Antaeus.*

"The Starlings," "The Drought," "Tampamachoco," "The First," "Antigua," "The Cellar," and "The Tale of Sunlight" appeared in *Poetry.*

The poems "At the Cantina" (1976), "The Map," "The Little Ones" (1977), and "The Shepherd" (1978), copyright © by The New Yorker Magazine, Inc., in the respective years shown.

for the two families

Those that went away . . . those that stay

CONTENTS

EL NIÑO

The moment he stepped out
Of the spark
Struck from a rock,
Our old yard opened
Like a curtain
And what appeared was what I lost
Years back.

        He nodded follow,
And I followed, walking
In a flag of his shadow
To the peach tree
Bloated with blossoms.
With a stick, he tapped
The stone walk
Scuffed with a geography
Of strange markings,
And a wooden bench
Against the shed,
Sagging under a weight
Of all the rain
It had swallowed.
He tapped the incinerator,
Its strata
Of buckled cans
And bottles that burst
And froze
In a heaven of ash.

It grew cold.
The air twisted thick
As a wet towel.
A grayness swung
Across the light,

3

And he kept moving
Through the yard,
Tapping *shovel, chinaberry,*
Train. He tapped
The dry spot
Where again I knelt and dug
For the magical ants
That vanished,
Link by link,
Into a cellar of chalk-dirt
And the untangled roots
Through which the dead leave.

THE POINT

The moon going orange
Through a cloud
That refuses to move,
Molina in the yard
Talking to a chicken
That blinks with eyes
Blown deep
As targets. It circles
Its droppings
And says nothing
Of the wind that passes
Through a door
Nailed shut
By its own poverty;
Or of the galaxy
Of lint tilting on its axis,
Those unmapped stars
He counted twice
And named for his country.
Why the cloud
That never rained,
The sleep that is something
More than sleep?
Why the crow found
Flat as a glove,
Its beak open on a yawn?
Nothing answered,
He weighs six rocks
Against his hunger
And bursts a streetlight
That won't come to the point:

The sky swallows
Hard on the echo
And Molina's eyes are lost
Between the blue of two stars.

THE MAP

When the sun's whiteness closes around us
Like a noose,

It is noon, and Molina squats
In the uneven shade of an oleander.

He unfolds a map and, with a pencil,
Blackens Panama

Into a bruise;
He dots rain over Bogotá, the city of spiders,

And x's in a mountain range that climbs
Like a thermometer

Above the stone fence
The old never thought to look over.

A fog presses over Lima.
Brazil is untangled of its rivers.

Where there is a smudge,
Snow has stitched its cold into the field.

Where the river Orinoco cuts east,
A new river rises nameless

From the open grasses,
And Molina calls it his place of birth.

THE TRACKS

Because Molina ladders
A chinaberry
In the morning
He is a sloth
That hangs like smoke
By ten fingers
And the luck
Running along his palms;
I'm the possum
Yawning on a limb
That won't give
Under the heaviness
Of smashed windows,
Greased coats,
And hands frozen
To a rake
Refusing to scratch
The yard's back.
We are here,
Quiet, separated
From the language
That calls the day
To order, because earlier
Our fathers knelt
For the coin
Rolling under the bed
And our mothers
Fitted news clippings
In a shoe whose sole
Was flapping *good-bye*.
It was when the door
Closed on their shadows,
The rat sipped
On its whiskers,

And the ants unlinked
Their wisdom on crumbs.
After we climb down
And the sun up,
We are animals
That are nameless,
Without snout or tail,
Trotting in an orchard
Where we say
It is winter
And our tracks are lost
Under the snow
We called from the sky.

SONG FOR THE POCKETS

They carry the spoon that unearthed another tin spoon,
A magnet furred in iron filings,
A shag of lint.

They carry fiddle-neck and the arrow-face foxtail,
A harmonica grinning with rust,
The salt that forgot the palm it was rubbed from.

They carry the key whose door was burned,
A rattle of seeds capsuled in foil —
All that was lost in the street raised by its own rules.

THE SOUP

The lights off, the clock glowing 2:10,
And Molina is at the table drawing what he thinks is soup
And its carrots rising through a gray broth.

He adds meat and peppers it with pencil markings.
The onion has gathered the peas in its smile.
The surface is blurred with the cold oils squeezed from a lime.

He adds hominy and potato that bob
In a current of pork fat, from one rim to the other,
Crashing into the celery that has canoed such a long way.

Spoon handle that is a plank an ant climbs.
Saucer that is the slipped disc of a longhorn.
Napkin that is shredded into a cupful of snow.

THE LITTLE ONES

When fog
Stands weed-high
And sky
Is the color
Of old bed sheets,
Molina and I
Squat under an oak
On a bench of roots,
Burning paper
And leaves
To keep warm.
We blow into
Our hands
And the white
That comes out
Drifts upward
Where heat
Does not reach.
Our eyes glow
Before the fire,
And Molina says
The sparrows
In this tree,
The little ones,
Find their heaven
Where the sky
Meets the earth.
For days
They will point
Far into coldness
Until that cold
Becomes the dark
Blowing across

Their eyes.
They will know
The South
When a bundle of smoke
Moves against
The wind
And fields lift
The rains
Of a thousand years.

BLANCO

My sister comes, quietly,
Stepping where I step,
The street numb from the fog.
We are explorers.

          In our yard
With a flashlight on
And eclipsed by the cold,
We know the sun is lost to this,
The woodpecker to its whittle,
The worm to its stitch
That closed our father's grave.

And ear pressed to the ground,
My sister speaks of
Ants nibbling the pods unstrung
From eucalyptus,
Roots cradling the skull's smile.

Hands curled into binoculars,
I focus on
What is suddenly a house wrapped
In incense. Inside,
Our father at a table
Listening to us move
As the earth moves.

I spit into my sister's palms,
Rubbing them brown with the dirt
Pinched from our lives.
I point *over there,*

And linking her small hands
Into a telescope,
She centers on the white
He could step from, his voice clear
And burning a hole
Where this sky is once more . . .

THE WOUND

You ran home,
A five year old,
Past the yards
Frisked clean
Of sprinklers, fruit,
The TV antennas
That buzzed with a voice
From beyond this barrio,
Offering the wisdom of light bulbs.
You passed the old *Tejanos*
Porched in shade,
Watching the sky
For a blimp
To haul in the night
Or a miracle
To fall like rain
And become the rain
You once opened
Your hands to.
Home, you spotted iodine
On the bites
That puffed like braille
And waited for a fever
To climb upward
In a vein,
Sure as a compass.
You said nothing
And went to your room.
That night
In bed,
The radio howling
In the next room,
You lay awake,

Thinking of your body
Unruffling to earth
And what prayer
Could raise you, slowly,
From one dark place into another.

THE STREET

Then we would hardly eat except to be seen.
— Elio Vittorini

Through the first days of Lent
The widow lugs the town's wash outside
In the heat squatting

Among onions and tomatoes poled waist-high,
Chiles and the broken fingers of peas
That point down.

Waving off the chickens,
She pins the grayness to the line, and beyond
This line, in the same boredom
That drips from the wash,

The old rock
In a bench of shade, the old
Who have come here to suck their tongues
And stare at each other's shoes

South of what was never received.
                *

Molina shovels for what the earth gives,
Pulling up the barbed tooth
And the hooked nail,

A rug of pressed roots
Shook clean
And hung to dry in the open air.

He raises a lunch pail black
From the crossing of ants
And dips his arm
Into the hole, feeling the stones
Squat beyond the moon's tug.

When his flushed face
Is something to hold under a faucet,
Wring out like a towel,
It will be hours later.
It will be twilight.

It will be the child digging slowly,
But still digging,

While the night
Arrives with a wind
Clearing the way home.

*

Because a puddle has outstared the sun
And the shade has rearranged itself
Like furniture,

Julio, the retired butcher,
Sits under the full skirt of a willow,
Talking to the photo
Of his first wife,
Her face greased with a thumbprint
And caught in a lean year.

He opens his pocketknife, closes it.
He pulls a nickel from his coin purse
And without looking
Dates it a 1959 D,

And in '59 he rose
At daybreak
To pluck the chicken of its burst heart
And the maggots
That went deep as bullets
In the yellow of the pork's fat.

19

This world is silver, between two trees.
The light is folding
Like a stiff wallet, west of all
He has dreamed, miles from
The prayer that will close his eyes.
                    *

Goyo at the window, and no uncle
Arrives on the porch, to dust a coat
Or the boots spurred with foxtails,
Open at the tips.

                    No aunt comes,
Heavy-breasted, to bend over the sink
And gut a chicken of the two stones
It pecked from the yard.

The yard grows cold
And its light pulls away
At the speed it takes to shut a cupboard
Hiding the chipped saucer, a spoon bearded in lint.

Goyo goes outside, near the fence,
And watches his cat lick what is salted
Under each paw

                    for this hour
When the moon is a prop above the trees
And the streetlight assumes
Where its light falls
Someone should walk.

                    *

Barber or field hand,
Whore's brother, pickpocket's son,
They come, shoeless, to the ditch
Where the starlight maps the water

And the current moves
Against its pull,
Slowing this night.

          In the quiet
Between one cigarette
And another, they stand breathing
Chilled air, listening
To the reeds benched
Along the water,

The peacock and the pocked toad,
The cricket that ticks
Like fire.

If the weeds rustle,
It is the wind stones freed
At noon.

If a child sets a branch drifting,
It will sink eastward
Through a seizure of moonlight,
Past the unroofed houses,
Bearing his name
Which is always sent back.

    *

When the morning is a tablet
Of cold spit he cannot swallow,

Cruz leaves
For the Westside,
The neoned juke box and the warm beer
Sending up its last bubble,

For the cue stick
Swung hard against an ear, the mouth blooming.
A fly circles in the light,
And he orders a stronger drink.

Back home, he stands on the front porch
Before the window, his reflection,
A crack running
Like stitches

From one corner to the next.
He looks in as though this were not his
House and squints

Where the rat, nibbling what it can,
Turns once again to meet his stare.

      *

At *La Fiesta,*
The uncle drops a coin of blood
In each palm,

An offering for the basin
Where the water rises in a steam
He cannot see
And vanishes into a cloud.

The white woman over an electric range
Will not know the pain
That stiffens
Like a star in a second of full darkness,

Nor what makes him push
His gloved fist
In the windows that eat their echoes —

She can't even guess.

One could say a bottle
That emptied like a cough
Turned over, slashed at a face,
And later, a car tire.

One could say the wound tears again,
Opening like an eye
From a sleep
That is never deep enough.
          ❀
The poor are unshuffled cards of leaves
Reordered by wind, turned over on a wish
To reveal their true suits.
They never win.

        This means Theresa Fuentes,
Palm reader and washerwoman,
Stacking coins into vertebrae of silver
Fingered dull by the cold:

                Emilio Zaragoza pushing
Chorizo into sleeves of pig gut,
Roping them in threes along the wall:

Fat Mother Luisa threading
The needle's eye with sunlight
In a house of closed cupboards and open mouths.

So they continue, dark and unfamiliar,

Their children at a table,
Brother to his bowl, sister to her dish,
Eating only enough so as not to say good-bye.

THE CELLAR

I entered the cellar's cold,
Tapping my way deeper
Than light reaches,
And stood in a place
Where the good lumber
Ticked from its breathing
And slept in a weather
Of fine dust.
Looking for what we
Discarded some time back,
I struck a small fire
And stepped back
From its ladder of smoke,
Watching the light
Pull a chair
And a portion of the wall
From where they crouched
In the dark.
I saw small things —
Hat rack and suitcase,
Tire iron and umbrella
That closed on a great wind —
Step slowly, as if shy,
From their kingdom of mold
Into a new light.

Above, in the rented rooms,
In the lives
I would never know again,
Footsteps circled
A bed, the radio said
What was already forgotten.
I imagined the sun
And how a worker

Home from the fields
Might glimpse at it
Through the window's true lens
And ask it not to come back.
And because I stood
In this place for hours,
I imagined I could climb
From this promise of old air
And enter a street
Stunned gray with evening
Where, if someone
Moved, I could turn,
And seeing through the years,
Call him brother, call him Molina.

THE LEAVES

When the wind lifted
The raked leaves shuffled off
Like shoes
And left the street
For the dry place
Inside a cloud,
For the sparrow
That raises the sun.
Drifting, they
Rubbed the soft belly
Of earth, loosening
Its hold on rock.
Blown into fences,
They scattered
Like ants
And followed
What the ants followed
Through streets,
In small herds
Where no one pointed
Or stroked his beard.
They crossed orchards,
A stand of trees
They never saw,
Scratching an alphabet
In the damp ground.
Climbing the foothills
Under a rumor
Of rain,
The leaves left
For a new wind
That would fall
Through them like light

And the brightness
They would see
Was their own
As they moved south
Toward the jeweled fire of snow.

ANTIGUA

The heat standing tall as a door, you go outside
And drink from a tin dipper

Water so clear it holds the sky,
Mapping the blue and all that goes beyond.

It is dusk now.
It is the town with eyes of a sad mule.

You watch the dark become a backdrop
To hunger, the streetlight

A moon that will not pull west,
Dragging its light under the rule of another heaven.

You think of the bus
And the dust that trailed it like a cape,

The slashed mountains rung pale
With roads that climbed through a fever of new air.

Below, streams twisted through trees,
A mist balancing

On the unsleeved limbs,
While you rose even higher

With your twenty-four years
And the language that had no reason to follow.

TAMPAMACHOCO

Through this continent of old water
A dead trout twisted under the moon's half-eye
The crayfish limped along   dragging its huge glove
The silt fell through three stratas of light
The driftwood raised itself into a tree
The gray unhooked a leash of bubbles
The stone opened its eye to release a fire
When morning came   the sky refused to look our way

LITANY

after a Mexican prayer of the poor

Santa Miseria, a broom is in the corner, a spoon in my mouth?
Sweet tooth of San Cuilmas, a fly guards our cake.
Keyhole of San Pedro, feel for us in the dark.
Lion of San Marcos, what is under each paw?
Sash of San Juan, rope us into prayer.
Hood of San Roque, what did you catch?
Rosary of San Miguel, hang as we hang.
Clogged nostril of San Blas, a toothpick might do.
Compass of San Jorge, 2×2 is more than enough.
Burnt match of San Lucas, guide us home.
Suitcase of Santa Catarina, the donkey won't get up.
There is a shoe for each foot, a cuff for each wrist,
More plates than forks. Amen.

THE STARLINGS

If there were no stars to say something of the coming weather,
No quarter moon to see by,
The starlings would not go south but shiver like water
In the tall trees, their eyes narrowed on the wind.

Refusing the fog and the rain against leaves,
They would climb the branches of gray light
Until snow fell, and they fell, their feet raised
And showing through the white, twigs to grow a new year.

THE DROUGHT

The clouds shouldered a path up the mountains
East of Ocampo, and then descended,
Scraping their bellies gray on the cracked shingles of slate.

They entered the valley, and passed the roads that went
Trackless, the houses blown open, their cellars creaking
And lined with the bottles that held their breath for years.

They passed the fields where the trees dried thin as hat racks
And the plow's tooth bit the earth for what endured.
But what continued were the wind that plucked the birds spineless

And the young who left with a few seeds in each pocket,
Their belts tightened on the fifth notch of hunger —
Under the sky that deafened from listening for rain.

THE FIRST

After the river
Gloved its fingers
With leaves
And the autumn sunlight
Spoked the earth
Into two parts,
The villagers undid
Their houses,
Thatch by thatch,
And unplucked
The stick fences
That held grief
And leaned from the wind
That swung their way.
What the sun raised —
Squash and pumpkin,
Maize collared
In a white fungus —
They left, for the earth
Was not as it was
Remembered, the iguana
Being stretched
Into belts,
The beaver curling
Into handbags;
Their lakes bruised
Gray with smoke
That unraveled from cities.
Clearing a path
Through the forest,
A path that closed
Behind them
As the day opened
A smudge of its blue,

They were the first
To leave, unnoticed,
Without words,
For it no longer
Mattered to say
The world was once blue.

THE SHEPHERD

The grasses begin where he begins
The descent home,
A harp swung over his left shoulder,
The moon over the other.
At his waist, a small satchel
Of jicama and a long nostril of turnip.

Kin to the felled tree,
The collapsed stone,
The three-legged chicken pickled and showing
In a cellar of the poor,
He is returning at
The pace at which the sun untangles itself

By the moon's laughter,
The willow's desire to touch its feet.
There is no hurry, toss the trees.
Good Wood, Good Fire, fall the chinked coins of leaves.
Where he steps, the grasses rub
Their notched faces, whispering his name.

THE YEARS

You watch who could be Aleman
Returning home, his eyes blown clear as smokerings.
You give him the name Paco Garcia,
Second son to a janitor playing shuffleboard
With a clot of dust. You give him a limp
And a face that yellowed from the center outward;
A bundle of old lies that ride thin as a lozenge
On the tip of his tongue. The mismatched shoes

Of his childhood forgotten,
You point years back to a barrio and a voice
Opening a hole in the dark that goes beyond his birth.
There, a brujo reads his face like braille
For the greed that will lag two steps behind
And traces a finger over his brow
Where the lines will lengthen and cut deep.

HOW AN UNCLE BECAME GRAY

to Garcia Marquez

One day his room fluttered
Like a neon
With the butterflies
That had followed him,
A herd of vague motion
He came to think
Was a cloud spread thin
And bearing
A blank message of rain.
They settled
Along his sleeve
And linked each finger
With the scent
The wind's tongue
Forgot to lick.
They opened and closed
Their wings, revealing
The bright circles
That focused like pupils
On the pure light
That stares through
The trees and beyond
The drift of summers
Rivers still trace.
When he shrugged
Them from his shoulders,
Unhooked their antennas
From his beard,
They gave off
The silver dust
A coin couldn't match,
The silver that laddered
His sideburns,

Tipped his brows
With something like snow.
So this moment arrived
With its eyes open,
Streaking his pompadour
The color caught
Between two branches
On a winter day,
The clarity
He would embrace like a tree.

THE MANUEL ZARAGOZA POEMS

THE CREATURE

This morning something
Perched like a bird
On my left shoulder,
And was silent.
If I brushed it away,
It reappeared
Like a premonition.
If I ran,
It clawed deep
Into my coat,
My wool coat,
And closed its eyes —
Or what I thought
Were its eyes.
So, here I was
Walking the town
Perplexed like a priest,
My neck stiff
As a new beard,
And no friend
Waving ¡Hola!
That afternoon
I prayed and lit
A candle for the spirit
Of my wife
Dead two years,
And still this
Creature tightened
And yawned
Into my ear.
At supper in my room,
It ate my bread
And the handle
Of a sharp knife.

To that I said Enough!
And left hatless
For the cantina,
Where again the creature
Lay on my shoulder
Like the hand of someone
Bearing grief.

AT THE CANTINA

In the cantina
Of six tables
A woman fingers
The ear lobe
Of a bank teller.
It is late,
And this place is empty
As a crushed hat.
A galaxy of flies
Circles the lamp.
Manuel wipes the counter,
Flicking ashes
Onto the floor.
The voices of
That couple
With the faces of oxen
On a hot day
Reach over his shoulder
And vanish
Into the mirror.
Finally they leave
Without nodding good-bye,
His hand on
Her right breast,
Her thumb hooked
In his watch pocket.
Manuel locks up,
Uncorks a bottle
And sits at a table.
All night he drinks
And his hands fold
And unfold,
Against the light,

A kingdom of animal shadows —
The Jackal,
The Hummingbird,
The sleepy-eyed Llama,
An Iguana munching air —
While the rooster stretches
To the day not there yet.

GRACIELA

Wedding night
Graciela bled lightly —
But enough to stain his thighs —
And left an alphabet
Of teeth marks on his arm.
At this, he was happy.
They drank mescal
In bed like the rich
And smoked cigarettes.
She asleep
And the bottle empty, he hid
A few coins in her left shoe,
Earrings in the right.
They worked long hours
Hoeing crooked rows of maize.
Evenings she wove rugs
And embroidered curtains
To market in Taxco.
In short they lived well.
However in the seventh month
With child, her belly
Rising like a portion of the sun,
Something knotted inside her.
The ribs ached. A fever climbed.
Manuel summoned the Partera
And though she burned pepper,
And tied belts around
The stretched belly,
The child did not ease out.
Days later she turned
Onto her belly
And between her legs
Unraveled a spine of blood.

THE JOURNEY

Bloated on beans, squash,
Goat's milk, I left
Before dawn for Taxco
With a clock
Needing a new face
And God knows what.
I followed the river Calabaza
Brimming with weeds
And lizards
Until it stopped
Where stones climbed
Like a stairway
These terrible hills.
At noon, or close to noon,
The heat rising
To the level of the wind,
I saw an iguana flutter
From under a bush
And vanish into the ribs
Of a fleshless mule.
The crazy thing was smiling.
It is the truth, friend.
When I picked up the ribs,
Turned it over, shook
It like a child,
The iguana did not appear
Or even click its tongue.
So I went on, did not
Look back, but thought
That God was testing me.
I could expect a bush
To flare before my eyes
Or the sky to rain toads

And the umbilical cords
Of the newly born,
Pigeons to choke
In the noose
Of their own breathing
And fall from the trees.
So this was the world, at noon.

A FEW COINS

Now and then
Manuel, stunned with
The same bordom
Of an ant circling
A dirty spoon,
Has visions of wealth.
Say, for instance,
To form a circus:
Nude dancers, a midget
With minute genitals,
Monkeys boxing
For carrots,
All the ugly gathered
Under one tent.
The prize attraction
Is a rooster
With the command
Of several dozen words,
A Latin phrase or two.
Or last week
After a conversation
With a shovel,
He wanted to bottle urine
And peddle it
To the tourists
In Taxco, saying
It is the lake water
In which Virgin Olga bathed . . .
Sometimes he brags
He worked outside Toluca
For Americanos,
Shoveling stones
Into boxes.

One morning
He unearthed a salamander
Cut from bone, collared
With small holes
Where jewels shone.
He sold it
To a skinny gringo,
And in parting
With it, wept
And muttered like
A harelipped prophet —
Bird in the stupid tree,
Wink at me . . .
God above the tree,
Call me Manuel the genius —
And simply walked away.

NADA

I turn 40. The sun
Does not turn.
What odds
Favor a miracle?
A woman
To go through town
Asking for me.
When we meet
She says, "Manuel
You poor soul, how long
Has it been . . ."
But I tell you
There is only a cart
Waiting in the street,
The burrows sniffing
Their own dung;
Only the sound
Of a broom striking
Children.
I search my one good hand,
Turning it over
Like a letter,
Counting the moles
Along my arm.
I leave my room
And walk this
Dilapidated town,
The sun against my neck
Like a scarf,
And do you realize
What is here —
Dust, chickens plucking
Each other's eyes.

CATALINA TREVINO IS
REALLY FROM HEAVEN

                    Last night
At Mother Tomas's,
We danced the
Chicken-with-its-head-chopped-off,
Her hands on my buttocks,
My crotch puffed
Like a lung
And holding its breath.
This wonderful woman
Stitched my neck
With kisses
And told secrets —
The silverware she stole,
Her spinster aunt
Living in Taxco, a former lover
With a heart condition.
I in turn, being educated
And a man of
Absolutely no wealth,
Whispered a line
Of bad poetry
And bit her left ear lobe.
Afterwards we left
Arm in arm
For my room, for our clothes
Piled in a chair, and she
Fingering my bellybutton,
I opening her
Like a large Bible,
The kingdom of hair.

THE RING

Sweeping the floor
I find a ring
Caught in a tiny bush
Of lint and hair,
A ring with no inscription
Or stone. However
It is gold
And could belong
To the grinning one
Who left
With two women,
Two bottles of mescal,
A headache that
Will arrive
With the mail
And his wife striking
Him with a chair.
And there is some
Possibility
It fell from
The finger of
The ditch keeper
Or the old one
Who peeks through keyholes.
I do not rule out
The odds
It belongs to the retired sergeant
Who danced alone,
Went home alone
And kissed his arm good night.
No matter, no matter,
It is gold
I shall sell
To the dentist

Perhaps he
Will press it
Into the barber's
Two good molars
Or the chipped eyetooth
Of the widow
Who will again smile,
Drink late,
And shine with
What fire shines
Inside her.

THE VISION

Ah, to rise one morning
With the ability
To strum a guitar
And with a voice
To say, "Hola, mi Novia,"
Would be everything.
I am speaking of
Entering Hotel Avila
Where my drunk compadres
Applaud like hammers,
Where a scarf of smoke
Falls in their beer,
And I climb onto
A small stage.
The room quiets.
Tuning the guitar
I notice Senorita Pacheco
Trying to be noticed,
Her legs crossed
And pumping
Softly like water.
I smile, light a cigarette.
She sips her drink.
I place the guitar
On my knee, flick
The cigarette,
And I play, brother, I play.

THE TALE OF SUNLIGHT

Listen, nephew.
When I opened the cantina
At noon
A triangle of sunlight
Was stretched out
On the floor
Like a rug
Like a tired cat.
It flared in
From the window
Through a small hole
Shaped like a yawn.
Strange I thought
And placed my hand
Before the opening,
But the sunlight
Did not vanish.
I pulled back
The shutters
And the room glowed,
But this pyramid
Of whiteness
Was simply brighter.
The sunlight around it
Appeared soiled
Like the bed sheet
Of a borracho.
Amazed, I locked the door,
Closed the windows.
Workers, in from
The fields, knocked
To be let in,
Children peeked

Through the shutters,
But I remained silent.
I poured a beer,
At a table
Shuffled a pack
Of old cards,
And watched it
Cross the floor,
Hang on the wall
Like a portrait
Like a calendar
Without numbers.
When a fly settled
In the sunlight
And disappeared
In a wreath of smoke,
I tapped it with the broom,
Spat on it.
The broom vanished.
The spit sizzled.
It is the truth, little one.
I stood eye to blank eye
And by misfortune
This finger
This pink stump
Entered the sunlight,
Snapped off
With a dry sneeze,
And fell to the floor
As a gift
To the ants
Who know me
For what I gave.

THE SPACE

West of town,
Near Hermosa's well,
I sleep sometimes —
In a hammock of course —
Among avocado trees,
Cane, spider-grass,
The hatchet-faced chula,
The banana's umbrella
Of leaves.
It is here
In the spiny brush
Where cocks gabble,
Where the javelina
Lies on its side
Like an overturned high-heel.
I say it is enough
To be where the smells
Of creatures
Braid like rope
And to know if
The grasses rustle
Is only
A lizard passing.
It is enough, brother,
Listening to a bird coo
A leash of parables,
Keeping an eye
On the moon,
The space
Between cork trees
Where the sun first appears.

PITT POETRY SERIES

Paul Zimmer, General Editor

Shirley Kaufman, *The Floor Keeps Turning*
Shirley Kaufman, *Gold Country*
Abba Kovner, *A Canopy in the Desert: Selected Poems*
Paul-Marie Lapointe, *The Terror of the Snows: Selected Poems*
Larry Levis, *Wrecking Crew*
Jim Lindsey, *In Lieu of Mecca*
Tom Lowenstein, tr., *Eskimo Poems from Canada and Greenland*
Archibald MacLeish, *The Great American Fourth of July Parade*
Peter Meinke, *The Night Train and The Golden Bird*
Judith Minty, *Lake Songs and Other Fears*
James Moore, *The New Body*
Carol Muske, *Camouflage*
Gregory Pape, *Border Crossings*
Thomas Rabbitt, *Exile*
Belle Randall, *101 Different Ways of Playing Solitaire and Other Poems*
Ed Roberson, *Etai-Eken*
Ed Roberson, *When Thy King Is A Boy*
Eugene Ruggles, *The Lifeguard in the Snow*
Dennis Scott, *Uncle Time*
Herbert Scott, *Groceries*
Richard Shelton, *The Bus to Veracruz*
Richard Shelton, *Of All the Dirty Words*
Richard Shelton, *The Tattooed Desert*
Richard Shelton, *You Can't Have Everything*
Gary Soto, *The Elements of San Joaquin*
Gary Soto, *The Tale of Sunlight*
David Steingass, *American Handbook*
David Steingass, *Body Compass*
Tomas Tranströmer, *Windows & Stones: Selected Poems*
Alberta T. Turner, *Learning to Count*
Alberta T. Turner, *Lid and Spoon*
Marc Weber, *48 Small Poems*
David P. Young, *Sweating Out the Winter*

0 00 02 0455013 1

MIDDLEBURY COLLEGE